Polka-Dot Puppy

by Jane Belk Moncure
illustrated by Helen Endres

Published by

Mankato, Minnesota

GROLIER

Your partner in education

Distributed by Grolier, Sherman Turnpike
Danbury, Connecticut 06816

The Library — A Magic Castle

Come to the magic castle
When you are growing tall.
Rows upon rows of Word Windows
Line every single wall.
They reach up high,
As high as the sky,
And you want to open them all.
For every time you open one,
A new adventure has begun.

Lisa opened a
Word Window.
Here is what she read.

Polka-dot Puppy did not have a home.
He sat all alone on a busy street corner.

Lots of people passed him by. But
no one gave him a pat or a smile.

Polka-dot Puppy looked for a home.
He looked in the window of a bakery.

He saw cookies . . .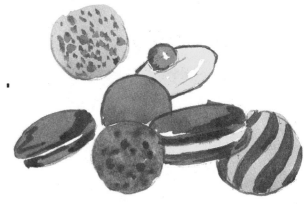

 and cakes . . .

and apple pies.

"Maybe a bakery is the place for me,"
said Polka-dot Puppy, wagging his tail.

But when he tried to go inside, the baker said, "Go away. Go away."

So Polka-dot Puppy went down the
busy street until he came to . . .

a toy store. He looked in the window.

He saw toy animals, toy cars,

dolls, and balls.

"Maybe a toy store is the place for me," said Polka-dot Puppy.

But when Polka-dot Puppy
tried to go inside, the storekeeper
said, "Shoo. Shoo. Out with you."

Then Polka-dot Puppy went next door
to a grocery store.

He looked in the window of the grocery store. Guess what he saw?

16

Hamburgers

and hot dogs,

milk

and cheese.

"Maybe a grocery store is the place for me," he said. Polka-dot Puppy rolled over.

When he tried to go inside, the
storekeeper said, "See the sign.
No dogs allowed."

Just then a little girl came by. She gave
Polka-dot Puppy an animal cracker.
"Poor puppy," she said.

It was getting dark, so Polka-dot Puppy
sat down in the doorway of a tall
building all alone.

The night watchman came by.
He gave the puppy a pat on the
head. "Poor puppy," he said.

After a while, it was very dark.
Polka-dot Puppy could not see much.
But he could hear. And he could smell.

Pop! Crackle! Pop! What was that?
Sniff! Sniff! Polka-dot Puppy sniffed
the air. He smelled smoke.

Polka-dot Puppy looked up.
He saw a fire in a window
way up high.

Polka-dot Puppy began to bark. He barked and barked so loudly . . .

that the night watchman
heard him.

When the watchman
saw fire, he
rang the
alarm.

A fire truck came down the street and
stopped right by the burning building.

In no time the fire was out.

"This little puppy saved the building," the night watchman said.

"Whose dog is he?" asked Fire-fighter Joe.

"He doesn't belong to anyone," said the night watchman.

"He does now," said Fire-fighter Joe. "The fire station is just the place for a fire-fighter pup.